Interview With The Ego

Shawn Henry

Presentation by *BookLeaf Publishing*

Web: www.bookleafpub.com

E-mail: info@bookleafpub.com

ISBN: 9789357444972

First edition 2022

DEDICATION

Dedicated to my loving and supportive family, as well as my amazing friends who have allowed me to grow alongside them. Even when I was at my worst, you stuck by me and reminded me that love was always there. I thank you.

PREFACE

Not many will admit this openly, but the road to self-healing is a lot more difficult than these TV shows and big Hollywood blockbusters make them seem. It's not always luxurious getaways and retreats where one seems to find themselves while entertaining hot and steamy affairs, or indulging in exquisite five-star meals from world-famous chefs like Gordon Ramsey himself. In all actuality, self-healing includes a lot of mental and emotional breakdowns, constant questioning of one's self and their role in the chaos surrounding them, confusion and a possible loss of direction, and various other "ugly" and "negative" qualities that would make even the strongest individual buckle down in fear.

However, as bad as it all sounds, there is a silver lining that comes with doing the work to properly heal. You become an even better version of the person you once were, someone confident enough to chase the life you not only want but deserve. Someone who stands in their power and sees all negative occurrences as a chance for lessons and growth, rather than immediately falling prey to a "victim" mentality.

Someone your inner-child would've needed and would feel proud to know that they will eventually become.

In this book, I share with you my own journey towards inner healing. Acknowledging that even during the worst of times, I was steadily learning more about myself and finding gratitude within the positives in my life, rather than letting every single bad thought about myself or the world around me completely consume and destroy me from the inside out. Though things may suck at times, there is always something to be grateful for if you choose to look close enough. There is a certain power had in shifting one's mindset from loss to abundance, and I aim to help everyone see that they are not alone on their journies of self-discovery.

Let this book be a reminder that, even when things seem their most bleak, there is always a light at the end of the tunnel. And that allowing yourself to heal can turn out to be the best thing you've ever done for yourself.

Venom

Building in my system,
I carry a weight that not many people can see.
A future tragedy waiting in the wings, my eyes
sting
as I shed my rose-colored glasses for those
surrounding me
and sadly, something needs to change.
Rearrange these thoughts, I sought to find a
balance
against the malice circling my lively hood,
concluding that
some emotions are not that of my own.
Outgrown, parts of my identity fall away in
decay,
as I grasp at loose strings of content
knowing that there's a darkness I haven't vent.

Apathy

Self-Growth is the key to inner peace.
Yet somehow my lesson is to release
the one characteristic I prided myself on the
most.
Detachment works best when you no longer let
emotions
linger on your chest, or in your mind, as over
time I have become
selfish with mine.
I fear that as I grow more self-aware, I'll lose the
ability to care,
and when someone asks for my heart, the pieces
won't be there.
It seems I've overshared.
In more ways than one,
being the therapist friend isn't fun, when the
name of the game is blame
rather than self-contain.
If everyone is the victim, then who's pulling the
trigger?
Problems just getting bigger and bigger,
as people perpetuate their own misery, because
apparently
those red flags look a lot like Six Flags if you
ignore them enough.

That's tough. No cap, I'm not trying to attack,
I'm just stating facts
and keeping it real about how I feel when I deal with
the back and forth so frequently.
A bunch of "he said, she said," but everyone goes deaf when
they're the ones being read.

I think it's time for me to go to bed.
Less I take the bullet for someone else when my
help is turned back against me. My word isn't
law, and it's not like I saw the future
or the past, just repeating back what I'm asked
like one's own mirror.
But maybe I should start being a little clearer.
A little more see-through, giving a preview of what it looks like
when I truly stop giving a fuck.
And by then, you'll be shit out of luck.

Slur

Words were always my weapon of choice.
Holding power in my voice, I tried to explain
The pain that sat in my brain, releasing years of
tension
so I don't go insane.
But like a train, I was derailed by one little
phrase.
Uttered in a blaze of passionate anger,
She flipped a switch by associating me
with a "bitch,"
and referring my behavior to that of
"A bundle of sticks."

Silenced and shattered, I'd gathered that I wasn't
the only
warrior with the "way of the tongue."
Just my purpose was to vent and hers
meant to stung.

About Me - Hurt

Your heart is heavy.
Burdened by the words left unsaid,
you've dealt with dread,
for the last several years of your life.
An inner strife rooted in a dead silence,
you've let violence of the mind
stop any trace of love and peace
from forming.
Internal mourning of the soul,
fear clings like mold that you'll get your
heartbroken yet again, when you let someone in,
whether that be family, lover,
or friend.

Escapism

Logout
Like a video game getting reset,
I must de-stress the distress
This reality has captured me
In without an ounce of warning.
I'm mourning,
The loss of a certainty
That was once clear to me
But now gasps in agony
And utter confusion
From the broken delusion
That I actually knew what I was doing...
I can't pre-tell
If this will all end well
So I'm going through the motions
Like I'm dancing on eggshells.

I just need things to be simple.
But like some kind of ripple effect,
I can't seem to dissect,
Where things stopped working properly.
It's odd to me,
That these words can flow so easily,
Only after some unknown mental tyranny.
How this no sex can make me a-sex,

When I'm just not in love yet,
But I fear the instant reject,
From the part that makes me suspect.
Why the rhythm of my feet,
Doesn't match the rhythm of my heart,
And my pen on this paper,
Has started to fall apart.

Nothing makes sense,
And I can't figure out why.
I need to fix up this console,
Need to find some kind of retry.

Bad Day

This little number right here is coming straight
off the dome.
Sometimes I feel like I should just stop letting
my mind roam.
It wanders away a bit too much for its own good.
And while I should be able to police my own
damn thoughts,
this inner battle for peace of mind is one that
shall be fought and fought.
I'm a whirlwind of emotions that seem to
operate on a mental plane.
Somehow unlocked my third eye and, like
Drake, nothing was the same.
Sometimes I think what I feel, and sometimes I
feel what I think.
Most times it all comes flowing out of me like
the drain of a kitchen sink.
Overwhelmed in my spirit, you'll find me down
in the dumps.
Like fighting Tyson or Ali, I'm left battered,
beaten, and bruised...like a chump.
I'll be like "Fuck, now I'm stuck. I can't figure
this shit out."
My brain be working overtime like celebs on
Twitter chasing for clout.

See, I really want to be happy. And often days,
this stays true.
Then some instance of profound sadness or
anger bathes me in red and blue.
Lie that I woke up on the "wrong side,"
sometimes it's easier that way.
Better half-assed excuses, than putting into
words what I can't say.

It's Too Much

Infinite souls lost in time
So many things like the thoughts
On my mind.
I'm a spirit of emotion,
Driven by passion and
Haunted by a deep lust
For something, I'm not even sure of.
They're things I want to say,
But I can't seem to articulate,
Everything that I contemplate,
When my heads spinning like a dinner plate in a
microwave that just burned out.
Damn...
I really wanted that sandwich too.
Kind of like how I want yo-
Wait, no, stop, restrict
"Girl, I know you want this dick!"
Now my thoughts are on the music
And not on your lips
That keep catching my eyes
Without a reason why.
I want this to end
Without losing a friend.
But I can't help but feel
This whole thing is unreal

Because when I said I was in love
I expected a shove,
A hit,
A diss,
But got none of the above.
Just some kind-hearted words
And a couple of smiles
Now I'm all confused
Is this all worthwhile?

The Warning

The other shoe finally dropped and my heart's
been torn asunder.
I sometimes wonder if Cupid enjoys playing me
for a fool
like I'm some kind of tool
that's here to mend others...
Meanwhile, I'm left to suffer.

Love doesn't live here.

Open-hearted, I embrace the chance
that romance will find me somewhere deep
down in my darkness.
Regardless of the lack of light that
continues to feel me with a fright
so strong that I no longer know what
Cupid's arrow even looks like.

But it be like that, right?

The hopeless romantic craving the antics
of something, he has never known.
Exploring the realm of the heart and discovering
things that the movies have never shown.
That "one, two, three, love comes easy"

set up is just TV magic.
End of the day of it all goes like a Shakespeare
play: Tragic.

The Cycle

An attempt at honest communication
in a world of hyper self-extension.
Fighting a battle that can't be won without
thoroughly unpacking the family tension.

I approach, open heart and open-minded,
seeking some form of parental guidance,
but am left feeling weaker and voiceless,
more so than if I would've just sat in silence.

Picking apart myself, word by word,
the thought that I may have done something
wrong.
Distrusting my version of reality,
self-uncertainty creeping up the more this
continues to prolong.

Like a red thread of fate, twist and turns make it
harder to see where it originates.
Watching one person's pain cause a chain
reaction in which I'll soon resonate.

Speaking my truth involves an exploration of
trying to find the bigger picture.

The ingredients that were placed together before
I was even added to the mixture.

Dynamics that need to be broken, ones proving
themselves detrimental.
Negative patterns being passed on,
families become like celebrities:
influential.

Working up my nerves to "break the habit" like
Chester from Linkin Park.
Wondering which I fear more from this beast:
it's bite or it's bark?

The Working Man

A cog in the machine that's constantly being
overused.
Too many tasks at once, this is major program
abuse.
Son, brother, cousin, and make-shift man of the
house.
Pushed and pulled left and right, nagged daily
like I've got a spouse.

I see all the issues, so many you'd think I'm here
collecting comics.
Don't need to study too much to figure out these
bizarre family economics.
I believe I can fix it, be the GEEK, the problem
solver.
But this stress got me vexed like I'm the world's
youngest father.

Smoked Out

Passenger seat, windows low,
Memories come and go.
They flow, like water,
Up the headphones, through the wires,
Traveling higher and higher
Into my brain. Insane,
How a set of beats and hooks,
Can have you so shook,
So chilled, revealed the inner thoughts
You keep, that sleep
But are awakened
by the rhythm in your ear
And murmur in your chest
I stress and confess
that somewhere deep down
I am truly, truly, vexed.

BullSh*tting

I present to you, in the clearest of views, an
absence of thought.

A blank canvas of opportunity waiting
expectantly for some abstract confession of my
identity or a memory infused with the resonance
of...something.

Nothing plagues me more than this irate desire,
that goes without tire, in pursuit of artistic
expression beyond feelings of depression or
whatever's exposed in an emotional session.

In all honesty, I'm a little bit stuck.

Hoping that with my luck, this nonsensical purge
of words will curb this urge to create a piece of
content worth feeling content about.

Man, I hate writer's block.

Release

Breath hitches and deep wishes,
Intimacy mixed with devotion,
Lust filled stares plaguing me,
Rocking the boat in the ocean.
Solo player on the joystick,
Stress relief in the after-hours,
Daily games of cat and mouse,
Ending with nothing but cold showers.
Deep craving for sensual touch,
A partner, a player two.
Forbidden thoughts running rampant,
Turned on by the taboo.

A New Level

Tapping into my mental,
I start to see visuals
of my potential,
skyrocketing higher than anything
I ever thought imaginable.

Some inner flame that
blazes bright and burst up like a
Phoenix. And I mean this,
when I say you might need a Kleenex
after witnessing my
artistic genius.

My power grows, reaching over
nine thousand. Arousing
suspicions that my origins are
something other than earthly.
But am I worthy,
of a cosmic backstory?

Searching within, I can't
pretend that my energy hasn't
been hitting different lately.
So maybe, I'll ride this wave
that's seeming to pave

the way to a destiny I haven't
foreseen.

Does this mean, I'll have to
come out of this shell?
Potentially find myself at
the gates of hell?
Fully explore what I love up
until my heart swells?
The only answer I conceive
appears to be...
"Oh well."

The Story-Teller

Heartfelt letters mesh together
to set my heart ablaze.
Tender touch of pen on paper,
putting the mind in a haze.
It's warm embrace,
lighting a fire, invoking desires,
of traveling far away.
Finding a place, some kind of space,
where my parts, my thoughts, can stay.
Playing with things,
locations and beings,
that only my eyes can see.
Exposing myself through somebody else,
how the world may seem to me.
Setting them free to grow and breathe,
crafting a life of their own.
Sharing stories of tragedy and triumph,
we speak like old friends on the phone.
In my zone, I'm the wordsmith,
a universe sits in my hand.
An untapped potential,
my powers are mental,
I just need myself to understand.

The Romantic

To understand me is to recognize
that I was born from a place of love.
Somewhere more mysterious than the clouds
formed in Heaven,
Or the shine of stars in the night sky
above.
A divine being reminiscent of the Greek deities
of Cupid and Eros.
Hell, I'd probably even do the work too if I
could just sprout wings,
find some damn magic arrows.

See, I believe in a romance that doesn't seem to
truly exist.
One that's pure and natural, void of way too
many conflicts.
One where "I say what I mean," and "you mean
what you say."
One where true love is what really matters at the
end of the day.

It's just, sometimes my thoughts seem to get the
best of me.
Having unsolicited dreams and visions of
someone who's supposed to be.

A mystery, forever shrouded in my fantasy.
Only time will tell who I'll eventually get to see.
My destiny.

Time Machine

Rewind the clock,
sit me down.
Immerse me in
a world of sound.
Of summer nights with TLC,
Bell Biv Devoe and some Heavy D.
Up the stairs, in my room,
the fire-escape balcony.
Man, back in '03,
this was the place to be.
Party jumping, music loud,
neighbors and strangers, in and out.
Food is frying, with drinks allowed,
best backyard jam, without a doubt.
A future vibe, a legacy,
something fixed in my memory.
I stay keeping good company,
it's in my family history.

Comfortable

Fairy tales don't cut it for me.
Stuck living in a fantasy, where
you and me (whoever you may be),
whether near or far,
naturally, fall together just like stars.
But that's wishful thinking.
I'm blinking, crust away from
sweet dreams and
imaginary movie scenes, that seem
so beautiful through romantic illusion,
but never quite there in real world
execution. Confusion, as to
what is love and how to find it,
while being reminded,
that the pursuit of love is
a never-ending journey that just
won't quit.

So, I'll just wait and see.
Hoping one lovely day,
someone will stop and say,
that things were meant to be,
And maybe then Cupid will point his
arrows at me.

Golden

A blue sky lullaby.

Clear eyes witness big lies
and grow up believing it's something
to live by. Unwise as these
dark clouds build up in their mind,
preventing them from seeing the
sunrise.

Black butterflies filling the chest
with feelings of protest
against the stress that this world
may present without any respect
for the person's consent. Hoping their
inner pain will drop and evaporate
like rain.

To be honest: things suck,
it's true.

But through and through,
we aim to prove that stormy weather
doesn't have to last forever. That like from
dusk till dawn, we must move on
and survive the flood until

its gone.

Those deep-rooted emotions,
don't run. It's not a crime.
Things will get better,
it just takes some time.
Let your hope soar high,
traverse how birds fly.
And let your heart become the light,
fueling that sunny sky.

Showtime

My love,
vibrating on a frequency unknown to thee
as a side of me awakens to creativity
and pleasure be my name if I don't embrace
this euphoric ecstasy.
Free of jealousy, I whole heartedly
explore a new version of my own identity.
One who seems to be obsessed with the
unseen, and I mean, that no longer does
my light dim, overshadowed to the brim,
with thoughts that my true self will fail.
I'll prevail, forward through the dark that's
stained my heart with fears of failure
in my endeavors to live a life that matches
the images in my head and the feelings
in my chest.
No longer repressed, I do what comes best,
opening myself up to whatever comes next.
I express, parts that have laid dormant
meet internal informants, telling them to get
ready for their grand performance.

Metamorphosis

Changes keeping coming without my consent,
Forcing me inward to make a descent,
Exploring the madness hidden deep within,
Crevices created and where they begin.
Breaking things down to build them back up,
I find answers in places that I was once stuck.
How a past full of conflict, like a venomous
sting,
Made a happy-go-lucky boy into a mentally
shattered king.
Facing an enemy that can't be physically
touched,
They don't tell you the path to healing can hurt
so damn much.
An untwisting of webs and storylines begin,
Ones of strife, heartbreaks, and loss,
Ones of love, happiness, and wins.
Connecting the dots, the many pieces to the
puzzle,
Finding the links to my fears and deep-rooted
inner struggles.
I sit with myself for the first time in years,
Let my walls come down and finally shed a few
tears.

Climbing out of the dark, things start getting
brighter,
Feeling fast on my feet, I find I'm vibrating
higher.
Like The Flash, I take off. Steady changing up
my future.
Now when things seem bleak, I can't help but
find the humor.